Contemporary

Foundations

Reading

Skill Workbook

Contents

Main Idea and Details 3
Time Order 7
Reasons 9
Facts and Opinions 11
Making Inferences from a Graph 13
Making Inferences from a Map 14
Making Inferences from a Cartoon 15
Making Inferences from a Photograph 16
Poetry 17
Poetry: Rhythm and Rhyme 18
Poetry: Imagery 19
Poetry: Simile and Metaphor 20
Fiction: Character 21
Fiction: Setting 22
Fiction: Plot 23
Fiction: Conflict 25
Fiction: Theme 26
Reading Review 27
Answer Key 29

Credits: **Cover** © Frank Tschakert/Alamy; **15** © Bettmann/CORBIS; **16** © RJ Matson.

www.mhcontemporary.com

McGraw Hill **Contemporary**

Printed in the United States of America.

Send all inquiries to:
Wright Group/McGraw-Hill
P.O. Box 812960
Chicago, IL 60681

ISBN 978-0-07-654861-3
MHID 0-07-654861-9

1 2 3 4 5 6 7 8 9 COU 12 11 10 09 08

Main Idea and Details

Follow these steps to find the main idea:

- Read the entire article.
- Find the topic. What or whom is the passage about?
- Find the main idea. What is the writer's most important point?
- Check that all details support the main idea.

Read the passage. Then write the main idea and the details that support it in the graphic organizer.

Clean Water for All

About one billion people in the world do not have access to a good water source. That is one-fifth of the world's population. Most of these people are poor people living in developing countries. The first problem is that the water they drink is often unclean. Unclean water causes many diseases. Nearly 5,000 people die every day because they do not have clean water. About 90 percent of them are under five years of age. Another problem is that some people must spend too much of their time carrying water for drinking, cooking, cleaning, and bathing. The women and girls are the ones who usually walk to water sources. Because of the time they spend carrying water, they cannot improve their lives by getting jobs or going to school. Several organizations are working to build clean water sources in villages. In recent years, billions of dollars have been invested in water projects. Everyone deserves a good source of safe water.

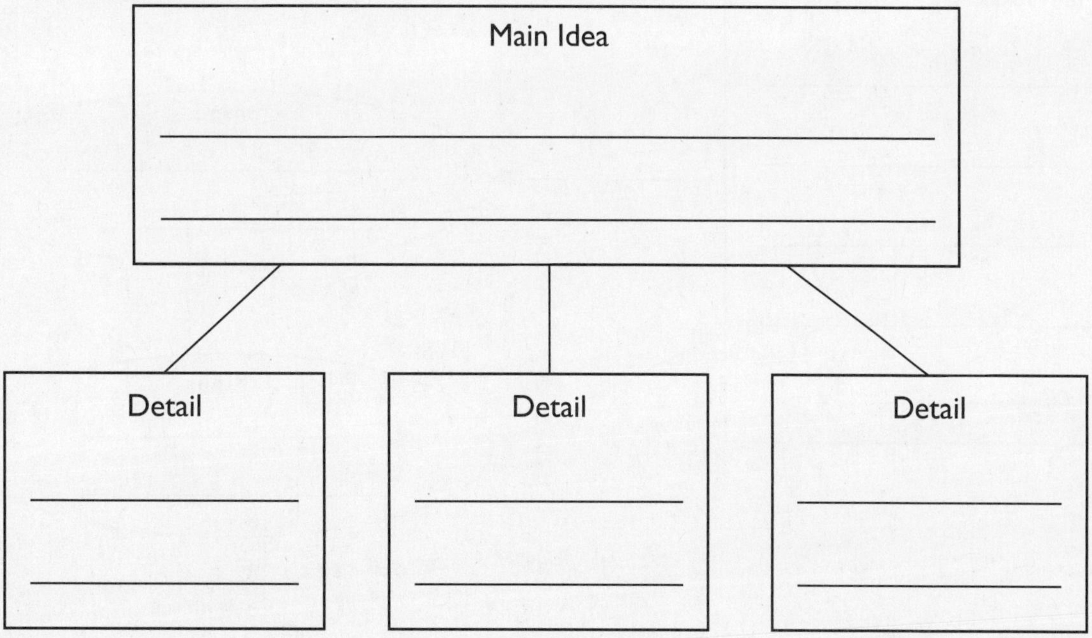

Main Idea and Details

Read the passage. Then write the main idea and the details that support it in the graphic organizer.

Great Gushing Geysers!

A geyser is a hot spring that can send water and steam shooting into the air. Three conditions are needed to make a geyser.

First, geysers must have a lot of water. Therefore, geysers are often near rivers or above underground hot springs.

Next, there must be a heat source. More than half of the world's 1,000 geysers are found in Yellowstone National Park, located mostly in the state of Wyoming. Much of the land in Yellowstone is inside an old volcano. When a volcano crater erupts and then collapses, a basin (called a caldera) is formed. The caldera in Yellowstone is 45 miles long and 30 miles wide. This old volcano heats water underground to make the geysers.

Finally, a plumbing system must be in place. The hot water needs a channel—or a pipe—that can carry the hot water to Earth's surface. This "pipe" must be tight enough to keep the water inside it. It must be small enough to create pressure so the water will shoot into the air when it reaches Earth's surface.

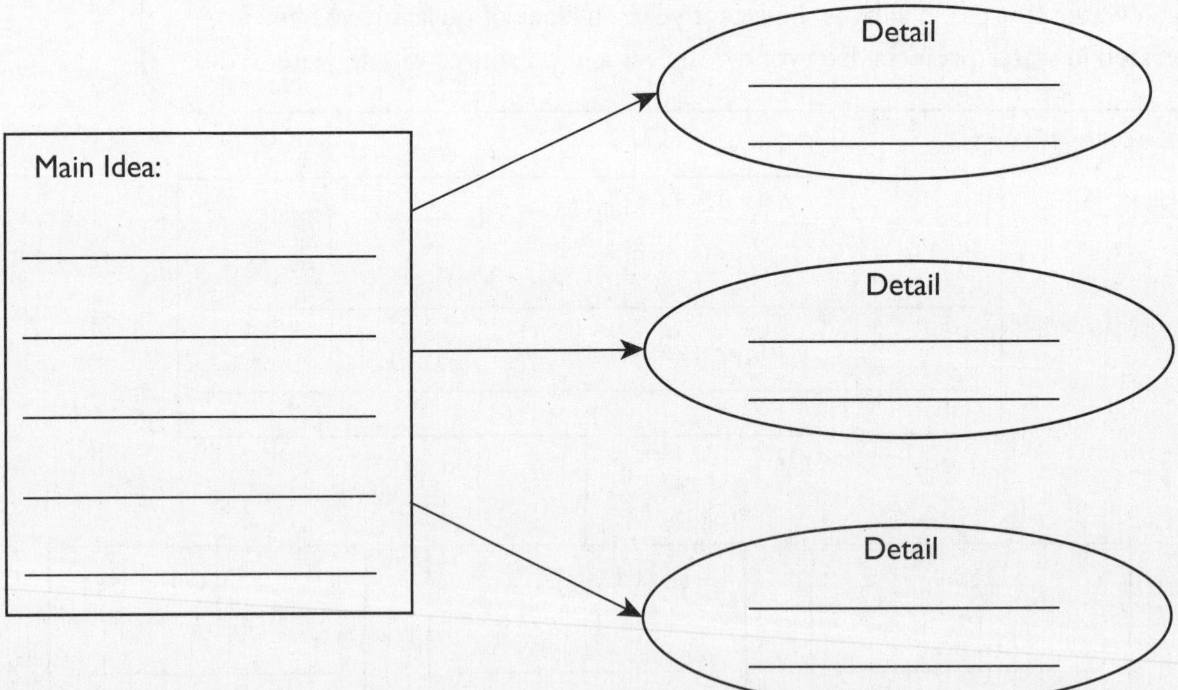

Main Idea and Details

Read the background note and study the graph. Then answer the questions.

Fresh Wind Blowing

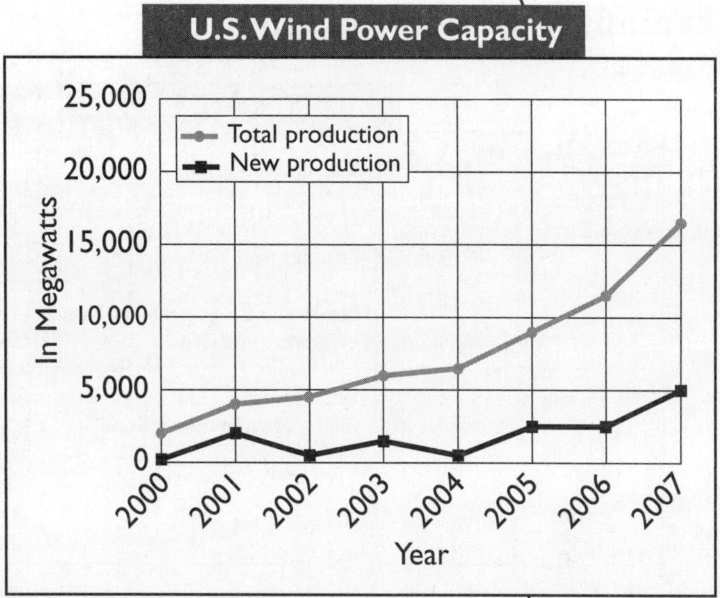

Background Note: Wind power is a renewable energy source. It is renewable because we will always have more wind. Wind power does not cause pollution. The electricity it produces is often cheaper than the electricity produced in other ways. More than 30 states now have large wind-power projects. Some people think that wind can produce as much as one-fifth of our energy needs. Farmers like wind power. They can earn money by leasing their land for wind farms. People who are interested in "green" energy can choose to buy electricity produced by wind. Such programs benefit Earth.

1. Write a sentence that states the main idea of the passage.

____

2. How would you describe the growth of wind power from 2000 to 2007?

____

3. What are three reasons for the popularity of wind power?

____

____

____

4. Why do you think wind power production is likely to continue to increase?

____

Main Idea and Details

Read the chart. Then answer the questions.

Comparing Two Revolutions

Comparison of Revolutions

Criteria	American Revolution	French Revolution
Was it a short-term success?	Yes. It freed the 13 English colonies from Great Britain. Yes. It set up a government based on democratic ideas.	Yes. It ended the French monarchy. Yes. It set up principles of democracy.
Was it a long-term success?	Yes. Its ideas are still the basis of the U.S. government in the 21st century.	Yes. Several times during the 1800s, France became a monarchy again; however, since the late 1800s, France has been a republic.
Did it have influence?	Yes. It influenced the French revolution and the revolutions in Latin America. Yes. It continues to influence the government of nations in the 21st century.	Yes. It influenced the revolutions in Latin America.

1. What is the main idea of the chart? ______________________________

____

2. What three criteria are compared in the chart? ______________________________

____

3. Give two reasons why the American Revolution was a short-term success. __________

____

____

4. In what way was the French Revolution not successful? ______________________________

____

5. In what part of the world have both revolutions had influence? ______________________________

Time Order

Study the time line and then answer the questions.

Culture and Science in the United States

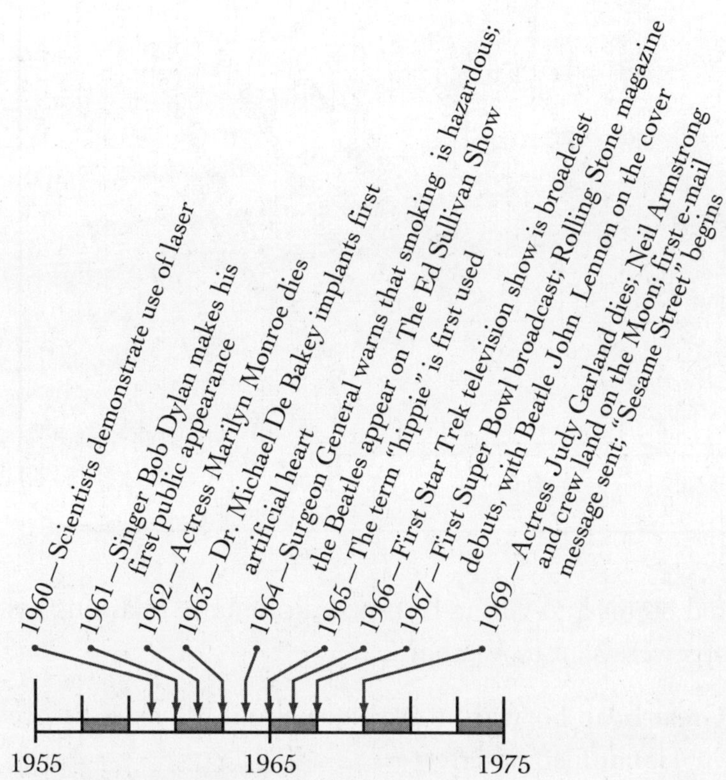

1. Which scientific invention occurred first—e-mail or the artificial heart implant?

____

2. During what year did four major events occur? ____________________

3. Which years featured one or more of the Beatles? ____________________

4. In which years did noted actresses die? ____________________

5. When were health warnings about smoking first given? ____________________

6. Which event occurred first—the use of lasers or the broadcast of *Star Trek*?

____

7. In which year did an important sports event occur? ____________________

8. Which similar events occurred in 1966 and 1969? ____________________

____

Time Order

Look at the time line. Then circle *T* if the statement is true or *F* if it is false.

Asia After World War II

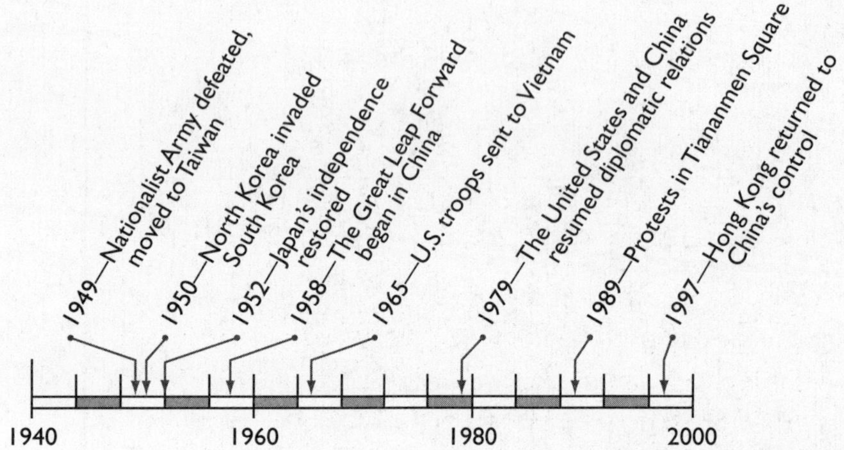

T F 1. The United States and China resumed diplomatic relations before U.S. troops were sent to Vietnam.

T F 2. China's Great Leap Forward took place about 30 years before the protests in Tiananmen Square.

T F 3. The invasion of South Korea occurred before Japan's independence was restored.

T F 4. Hong Kong returned to Chinese control in 1975.

T F 5. The United States sent troops to Vietnam 15 years after North Korea invaded South Korea.

T F 6. The time line shows that Asia was peaceful until 1949.

T F 7. Protests in Tiananmen Square took place only 10 years after China resumed diplomatic relations with the United States.

T F 8. The Nationalist Army of China was defeated after the Great Leap Forward began.

T F 9. The United States and China have always had friendly relations.

T F 10. The time line covers about 50 years.

Reasons

Use these steps to find the reasons why something happened:

- Read the entire article.
- Find the main idea, the writer's most important point.
- Look for words and phrases such as *because, since, therefore, due to,* and *consequently.* Reasons often follow these words.

Read the passage. Then write the main idea and the reasons that support it in the graphic organizer.

Saving the Rain Forests

The world's rain forests are being cut down at the rate of 95,000 square miles each year. This is an area about the size of the state of Florida. However, many groups are working to save these disappearing forests. There are several reasons why people want to protect the rain forests. First, more than half of all known plants live in rain forests, even though rain forests make up only about 6 percent of the world's land. These plants give off 40 percent of the world's oxygen. Second, plants take in carbon dioxide. This process helps prevent a buildup of carbon dioxide in the atmosphere. When carbon dioxide increases, more greenhouse gases are trapped close to Earth. Without the rain forest, global warming could increase rapidly. Finally, many medicines come from rain forest plants. Some of the diseases that these medicines treat include malaria and leukemia. An estimated 1,400 species of plants are thought to have chemicals that can cure cancer. If the rain forest is destroyed, these plants will never be harvested, studied, and used. Saving the rain forests should be everyone's business.

Main Idea	Reason 1
	Reason 2
	Reason 3

Reasons

Read the passage and answer the questions.

Heading Off Trouble

Wearing a helmet when riding a motorcycle saves lives and prevents serious injuries. The leading cause of death in motorcycle crashes is head injury. A motorcyclist who is not wearing a helmet is 40 percent more likely to die in a crash than a helmeted motorcyclist.

Motorcyclists who wear helmets save money if they are involved in a crash. Riders without helmets are more likely to have high hospital costs because they have longer hospital stays than helmeted riders. Their injuries are more severe, and they have more long-term injuries.

How well do helmet laws work? When Louisiana passed its helmet law, deaths dropped by 30 percent the first year, even though motorcycle registrations increased 6 percent. Similar percentage drops have occurred in other states.

Helmets are a motorcyclist's best protection from head injury. If you ride, regardless of the law in your state, wear a helmet.

1. What is the main idea of the passage? ______________________________

____

____

2. What are three good reasons for wearing a helmet? ______________________

____

____

3. What example shows that helmet laws work? __________________________

____

____

4. What is a motocyclist's best protection from head injury? ________________

Facts and Opinions

Determining facts and opinions are important reading skills.

- A statement that can be proved true is a fact.
- Opinions may include words or phrases such as *believe*, *feel*, *should be*, and *think*.
- Emotional words such as *fantastic*, *terrible*, and *wonderful* are often used in opinions.

Read the passage. Then circle *F* if the statement is a fact or O if it is an opinion.

Helping the Disabled

About 54 million people in the United States have a disability. Millions of these people could lead more active lives if they had motorized wheelchairs, hearing aids, or other modern equipment. However, many of these devices are very expensive. In 1990, Congress passed the Americans with Disabilities Act. This law promises that people with disabilities will have equal opportunities for education and jobs. Yet the law has not been fully enforced. I think this is terrible. We are too cheap as a nation to provide help. Congress should be doing more to make funding available.

Some of the changes that have been made for people with disabilities are helping other people as well. For example, people pushing baby strollers use the curb cuts designed for wheelchair users. Closed captioning on television helps people who are learning English as well as people who have difficulty hearing. Many people can benefit from simple changes. We should provide money and resources to help people with disabilities.

F O 1. About 54 million people in the United States have a disability.

F O 2. In 1990, Congress passed the Americans with Disabilities Act.

F O 3. This law promises that people with disabilities will have equal opportunities for education and jobs.

F O 4. I think this is terrible.

F O 5. We are too cheap as a nation to provide help.

F O 6. Congress should be doing more to make funding available.

F O 7. Some of the changes that have been made for people with disabilities are helping other people as well.

F O 8. We should provide money and resources to help people with disabilities.

Facts and Opinions: Bias

Read the passage. Then circle *F* if the statement is a fact. Circle *B* if the statement shows bias (that is, it unfairly presents only one side of an issue).

Pay-to-Play Is Unfair

My daughter has just come home with a list of fees for after-school activities. This year, the high school is charging students to play football, soccer, and field hockey. Students who play in the band or sing in the chorus must also pay fees. How can schools claim to offer a free education yet charge these fees? I'm sure this will mean that gifted and athletic students from lower-income families are going to be left out. They will not have the same happy memories of school that I have. We all know that the best way for people to learn to work together is by being on a sports team. Our society needs people who can cooperate, but many students will not be learning this skill. The note says that schools in 34 states charge students to be on a sports team. This pay-to-play idea is unfair. It means that some of the best players will not be on the team. What will happen to our powerhouse football team? We cannot let the Spartan pride down! We need to find a different solution to the funding problems of our schools.

F B 1. My daughter has just come home with a list of fees for after-school activities.

F B 2. This year, the high school is charging students to play football, soccer, and field hockey.

F B 3. Students who play in the band or sing in the chorus must also pay fees.

F B 4. I'm sure this will mean that gifted and athletic students from lower-income families are going to be left out.

F B 5. They will not have the same happy memories of school that I have.

F B 6. We all know that the best way for people to learn to work together is by being on a sports team.

F B 7. The note says that schools in 34 states charge students to be on a sports team.

F B 8. This pay-to-play idea is unfair.

F B 9. It means that some of the best players will not be on the team.

F B 10. We cannot let the Spartan pride down!

Making Inferences from a Graph

Follow these steps when making inferences:

- Look for clues that suggest what the writer is not stating directly.
- Analyze the clues to figure out what they mean.
- Test your conclusion against the facts given.

Read the background note and study the graph. Then answer the questions.

Inflation in the United States

Background Note: Inflation occurs when the cost of goods and services increases. Over time, a dollar buys less. If people's wages do not increase, they must purchase fewer items.

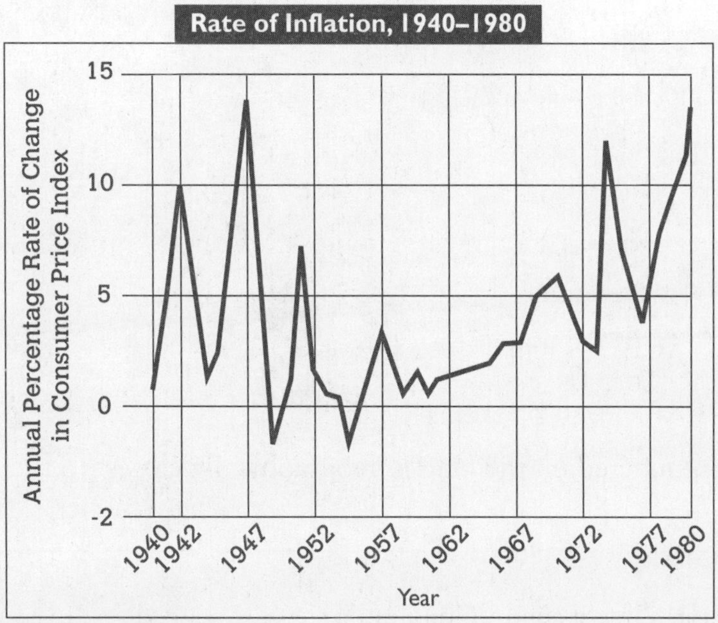

Source: U.S. Bureau of the Census

1. In what year was inflation highest? ______________________

2. When did inflation decline the most? ______________________

3. How would you describe inflation rates from 1970–1980? ______________________

____

4. Which period saw the least change in inflation rates? ______________________

5. What can you infer about inflation from the graph? ______________________

____

Making Inferences from a Map

Study the map and read the text box. Then answer the questions.

U.S. Intervention in the Caribbean and Central America After World War II

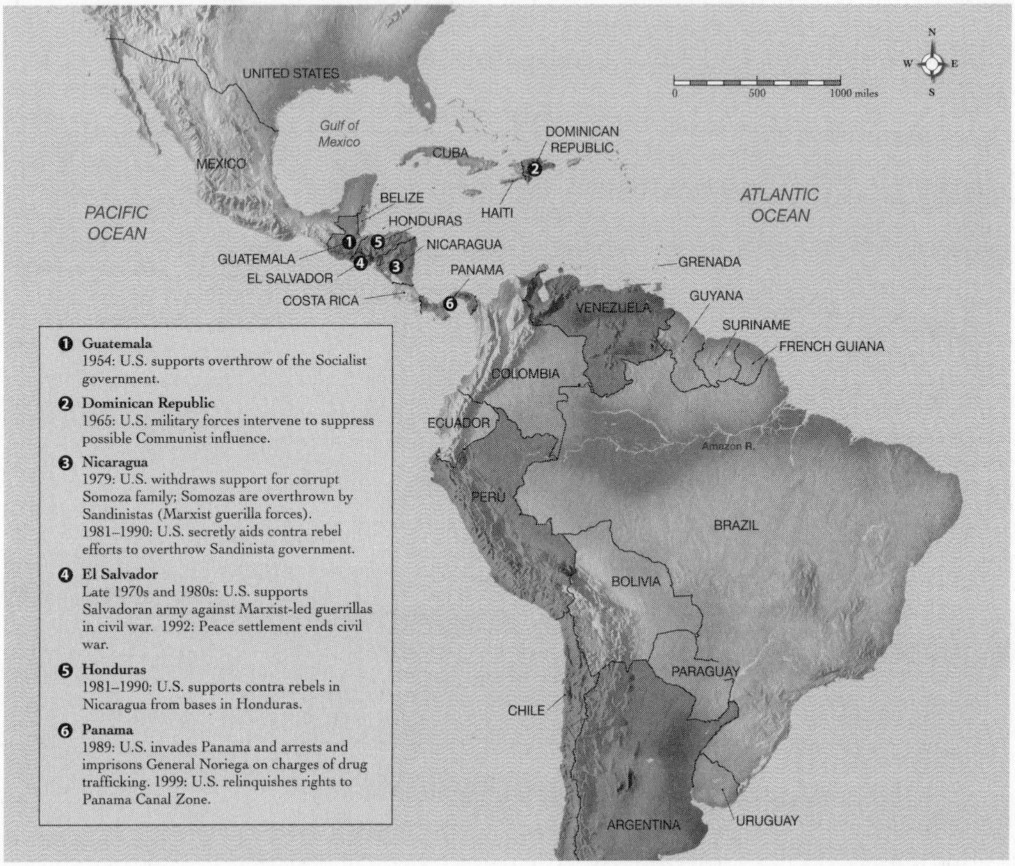

1. Which of the nations numbered on the map is geographically closest to the United States? ____________________

2. Why did the United States intervene in Guatemala? ____________________

____

3. In which country did the United States act secretly? ____________________

4. In which countries was the United States involved during the 1980s?

____

5. What can you infer about U.S. relations with Central American nations?

____

____

Making Inferences from a Cartoon

To understand the meaning of a political cartoon, it is important to identify the characters, subject, and the artist's opinion.

Read the background note and look at the cartoon. Then answer the questions.

What Should We Save?

Background Note: Lobbyists are people who try to convince members of Congress to vote in a certain way. They work for interest groups such as airlines or farmers. Many of their offices are on K Street in Washington, D.C. Lobbyists would probably say they are trying to help the country by solving problems.

"WHO SAYS THE AMERICAN PEOPLE AREN'T SAVING ENOUGH?"

1. What do the expressions of the people in T-shirts (the lobbyists) seem to suggest?

____

2. How does the cartoonist show that the lobbyists are businesspeople?

____

3. What are some of the causes these lobbyists represent? ______________________________

____

4. What is the couple at the left reading? ______________________________

5. What can you infer from the cartoon? ______________________________

____

Making Inferences from a Photograph

Read the background note and study the photograph. Then answer the questions.

He Stands Alone

Background Note: This photograph was taken in Tiananmen Square in 1989. This square is an important place in the center of Beijing, China. The ancient palace grounds stand nearby. In the middle of the square, the body of Mao Zedong (chairman of China's Communist Party from 1943–1976) lies in a glass coffin. Military parades and other large political events are often held at Tiananmen Square. It has also been the site of student demonstrations against the government.

1. What does the photograph show? ______________________________

____

____

2. What do you think was happening in China when this photo was taken?

____

____

3. What can you infer about the man in the photo? ______________________________

____

4. What do you think happened next? ______________________________

____

Poetry

Using these steps will help you understand a poem.

- Notice how the poem looks on the page.
  —Does the poem have a shape that helps you understand the poem?
  —Is the poem divided into stanzas (or verses)? If so, each stanza is probably about a different idea.
- Think about the mood of the poem, the feeling you have as you read it.

Read the background note and the poems. Then answer the questions.

Haiku

Background Note: Haiku is a form of Japanese poetry. A haiku is a three-line poem. Line 1 has five syllables, line 2 has seven syllables, and line 3 has five syllables. The ends of the lines do not rhyme. Haiku focuses on an image, usually an image found in nature. These two poems were written by Bashō, a famous Japanese haiku writer who lived in the late 1600s.

An old silent pond . . .
A frog jumps into the pond,
Splash! Silence again.

Temple bells die out.
The fragrant blossoms remain.
A perfect evening!

1. What is the image in the first poem? ______________________

____

2. Which two senses (sight, sound, smell, touch, taste) does the first poem appeal to?

____

3. In the first poem, what idea is found in lines 1 and 3? ______________________

4. What is the image in the second poem? ______________________

____

5. Which two senses does the second poem appeal to? ______________________

6. How many syllables are in the longest word in these poems? ______________________

7. What is the mood of these poems? ______________________

8. How does the writer create this mood? ______________________

Poetry: Rhythm and Rhyme

These hints will help you understand the rhythm and rhyme of a poem:

- Read the poem aloud, listening for the beat (or rhythm).
- Look for repeated words.
- Listen for rhyming words at the ends of lines and within the lines.

Read the poem. Then answer the questions.

An Old Story
by E. A. Robinson

Strange that I did not know him then,
That friend of mine!
I did not even show him then
One friendly sign;

But cursed him for the ways he had
To make me see
My envy of the praise he had
For praising me.

I would have rid the earth of him
Once, in my pride!
I never knew the worth of him
Until he died.

1. What pattern of rhyme forms at the ends of the lines? ____________________

____

2. What do you notice about the end words in lines 1 and 3 of each stanza?

____

3. How does the speaker of the poem say he felt about this friend? ____________________

____

4. When does the speaker begin to value the friend? ____________________

5. What do you think the title means? ____________________

____

Poetry: Imagery

These hints will help you identify the imagery in a poem:

- As you read the poem, look for words that appeal to your senses.
- Put yourself inside the world of the poem. Try to see, hear, touch, taste, and smell what is described in the poem.

Read the poem. Then answer the questions.

from "The Love Song of J. Alfred Prufrock"
by T. S. Eliot

The yellow fog that rubs its back upon the window-panes,
The yellow smoke that rubs its muzzle on the window-panes,
Licked its tongue into the corners of the evening,
Lingered upon the pools that stand in drains,
Let fall upon its back the soot that falls from chimneys,
Slipped by the terrace, made a sudden leap,
And seeing that it was a soft October night,
Curled once about the house, and fell asleep.

1. The speaker in this poem is describing fog as it curls around a house. What is the fog compared to? ____________________

2. List three actions described in the poem that help you visualize the fog.

   ____

   ____

   ____

3. What time of year and what time of day does the poem describe?

   ____

4. What words are repeated in lines 1 and 2? ____________________

5. What consonant sound is repeated in lines 3–5? ____________________

6. What consonant sound is repeated in lines 6 and 7? ____________________

Poetry: Simile and Metaphor

Poems create images that you can picture in your mind.

- Similes use the word *like* or *as* to compare two unlike things.
- Metaphors compare two unlike things without using the word *like* or *as.*

Read this poem about a flint (a stone that can be used to spark a fire). Then answer the questions.

Jewels
by Christina Rossetti

An emerald is as green as grass,
  A ruby red as blood;
A sapphire shines as blue as heaven;
  A flint lies in the mud.

A diamond is a brilliant stone,
  To catch the world's desire;
An opal holds a fiery spark;
  But a flint holds a fire.

1. In lines 1–3, the speaker of the poem uses similes to describe three jewels. What is each jewel compared to?

____

____

____

2. Complete this simile in your own words.

   A diamond is like a ______________________________

3. What is the rhyme pattern in the poem? ______________________________

____

4. How is a flint different from the jewels named in the poem?

____

____

____

Fiction: Character

Follow these steps to understand the characters in a story:

- Picture the characters in your mind as you read descriptions of them.
- Notice how the characters act, what they say, and how they say it.
- Think about what the characters say and think about one another.

Read the passage. Then fill in the graphic organizer.

A Meeting with a Convict
from *Great Expectations* by Charles Dickens

"Hold your noise!" cried a terrible voice, as a man started up from among the graves at the side of the church porch. "Keep still, you little devil, or I'll cut your throat!"

A fearful man, all in coarse grey, with a great iron on his leg. A man with no hat, and with broken shoes, and with an old rag tied round his head. A man who had been soaked in water, and smothered in mud, and lamed by stones, and cut by flints, and stung by nettles, and torn by briars; who limped, and shivered, and glared and growled; and whose teeth chattered in his head as he seized me by the chin.

"O! Don't cut my throat, sir," I pleaded in terror. "Pray don't do it, sir."

"Tell us your name!" said the man. "Quickly."

"Pip, sir."

"Once more," said the man, staring at me. "Give it mouth!"

"Pip. Pip, sir."

"Show us where you live," said the man. "Point out the place!"

	Pip	the convict
Physical Description		
How He Acts		
What He Says		
How He Says It		

Fiction: Setting

Follow these steps to understand the setting of a story:

- Look for words that tell you where the story takes place. Indoors or outdoors? City or country? A real place or a made-up place?
- Look for words that tell you when the story takes place. What year? What season? What time of day?

Read the passage. Then answer the questions.

The Perfect Room
Adapted from *Eight Cousins* by Louisa May Alcott

Rose walked to the middle of the room, stood still, and gazed about her with eyes that brightened as they looked, for all was changed.

This chamber had been built out over the library to suit some fancy, and had been unused for some years, except at Christmas times, when the old house overflowed. It had three windows, one to the east, that overlooked the bay; one to the south, where the horse chestnuts waved their green fans; and one to the west, toward the hills and the evening sky. A red sunset burned there now, filling the room with an enchanted glow; the soft murmur of the sea was heard, and a robin chirped "Good night!" among the budding trees.

1. What season of the year is it? How do you know? ______________________________

   ____

2. What time of day is it? How do you know? ______________________________

   ____

3. Where is the house located? ______________________________

   ____

4. How many windows are in the room? ______________________________

5. What can you tell about the house that this room is in? ______________________________

   ____

   ____

Fiction: Plot

Follow these steps to understand the plot of a story:

- Make a mental picture of the characters.
- Find the problem that the characters must solve.
- Identify the climax by asking yourself, "When is the problem solved?"
- Look for the conclusion, the event that brings the story to an end.

Read the passage. Then fill in the graphic organizer.

A Scare

Kara wasn't surprised to find the lump in her left breast. She knew, after all, that her grandmother had died of breast cancer. Two aunts had also had the disease. Still, she was afraid. She knew that she should get a mammogram, but she put it off. Every day she checked, hoping the lump would be gone. It never was.

"What's wrong with you?" Emily asked Kara one day at work. "You've been short-tempered and quieter than usual. What's going on?"

Kara took a deep breath. "I found a lump," she said. Kara was afraid to say the words aloud, but she needed to tell someone.

"Have you seen a doctor?" Emily asked.

"No."

"What are you waiting for? It's not going to go away on its own, you know. Besides, most lumps are benign. Come on, I'm walking you back to your desk, and you are making the call."

The next day Kara saw her doctor and had a mammogram. The doctor told Kara that she expected the lump to be benign, even with Kara's family history of cancer.

A few days later, Kara had a biopsy. Test results proved the doctor had been right. There was no sign of cancer. Kara took Emily to lunch to thank her for being such an encouraging friend.

Characters	Problem to Be Solved	Climax	Conclusion
Kara Emily the doctor			

Fiction: Plot

Read the passage. Then fill in the graphic organizer.

An Episode of War
Adapted from the short story by Stephen Crane

When the wound was disclosed, the doctor fingered it critically. "Humph," he said.

"You come along with me and I'll tend to you." His voice contained the same tone as if he were saying, "You will have to go to jail."

The lieutenant had been very meek, but now his face flushed, and he looked into the doctor's eyes. "I guess I won't have it amputated," he said.

"Nonsense, man! Nonsense! Nonsense!" cried the doctor. "Come along, now. I won't amputate it. Come along. Don't be a baby."

"Let go of me," said the lieutenant, holding back angrily.

And this is the story of how the lieutenant lost his arm. When he reached home, his sisters, his mother, his wife sobbed for a long time at the sight of the flat sleeve. "Oh, well," he said, standing shamefaced amid these tears, "I don't suppose it matters so much as all that."

Main Character	
Problem to Be Solved	
Climax	
Conclusion	

Fiction: Conflict

Follow these steps to identify the conflict (or problem) in a story:

- Look for the problem that the characters face.
- Decide whether the conflict is external (between a character and someone or something else) or internal (within the character's mind).

Read the passage and answer the questions.

Jane and Her Cousin John
Adapted from *Jane Eyre* by Charlotte Brontë

[This story is being told by Jane Eyre. She is an orphan who lives with her older cousin John.]

"What were you doing behind the curtain?" John asked.

"I was reading."

"Show me the book."

I returned to the window and fetched it.

"You have no business to take our books. You are a dependent, mama says. You have no money. Your father left you none. You ought to beg, and not to live here with gentlemen's children like us, and eat the same meals we do, and wear clothes at our mama's expense. Now, I'll teach you to go through my bookshelves—for the books ARE mine. All the house belongs to me, or it will in a few years. Go and stand by the door, out of the way of the mirror and the windows."

I did so, not at first aware of what his intention was. But when I saw him lift and poise the book and stand to throw it, I instinctively moved aside with a cry of alarm: not soon enough, however. The volume was flung, it hit me, and I fell, striking my head against the door and cutting it. The cut bled, the pain was sharp. My terror had passed its climax, and other feelings followed.

"Wicked and cruel boy!" I said. "You are like a murderer—you are like a slave-driver—you are like the Roman emperors!"

"What! what!" he cried. "Did she say that to me? Did you hear her, Eliza and Georgiana? Won't I tell mama? but first—"

He ran headlong at me: I felt him grasp my hair and my shoulder.

1. What is the problem that John faces? ______________________________

2. Is the conflict internal or external? ______________________________

3. How does John decide to solve his problem? ______________________________

4. What is Jane's response? ______________________________

5. What do you predict will happen as a result of Jane's response? ______________________________

Fiction: Theme

These hints will help you understand the theme of a story.

- Think about the lesson that the characters learn about life.
- Ask yourself, "What did I learn from this story?"
- Put the writer's message in your own words.

Read the passage. Then answer the questions.

Driving Toward a Dream

Juan had always admired his uncle Jorge. As a boy, Juan loved to ride in one of his uncle's big dump trucks. He could think of nothing better than owning and driving a big truck. As a young man, his only goal was to drive for his uncle's company. When he got his driver's license, he asked his uncle for a part-time job.

"No," his uncle said sadly. "Your mother tells me your grades are slipping. Your job right now is school. If you do not take that job seriously, you will never be a good employee. I don't need a lazy young man working here."

"But all I've ever wanted to do was drive a truck for you. I don't need good grades to do that," Juan protested.

"To work for me, you do," his uncle said firmly.

"All right, then. I'll show you that I am a good worker."

Juan stopped hanging around the garage. He studied harder, and his grades improved. One term he even made the honor roll. After Juan graduated, his uncle gave him a job. Later he went to junior college to learn more about business. He became part-owner of his uncle's company. Now Juan hires only hard workers—the ones who had good grades in school.

Part A Circle *T* if the statement is true or *F* if it is false.

T F 1. As a boy, Juan wanted to own his uncle's company.

T F 2. Juan's uncle refused to hire Juan because he wasn't doing well in school.

T F 3. Juan went to college to learn more about automotive maintenance.

T F 4. Juan eventually became part-owner of the trucking business.

T F 5. Juan will hire anyone with a high school diploma.

Part B

1. What is the external conflict in the story? ____________________
2. What is the internal conflict in the story? ____________________
3. What is the climax of the story? ____________________
4. State the theme of the story in your own words. ____________________

Reading Review

Part A Read the passage. Then write the main idea and the details in the graphic organizer.

Saving at the Grocery Store

With grocery prices rising, everyone is looking for ways to save money on food. Saving requires planning, clipping, and shopping smart. *Planning* means first writing down the week's menus. The next step is looking at the grocery ads in the newspaper or online. A smart shopper changes the menus to fit the sales. Make a list of what you will buy and stick to the list. *Clipping* means clipping coupons or printing them from the Internet. Using coupons at stores that already have these products on sale brings further savings. *Shopping smart* means buying store brands, which are usually less expensive than brand-name products. It means shopping at discount stores. It also means avoiding prepared foods. These foods are expensive, and they often have chemicals added to them. You can make tasty, healthy meals by using fresh vegetables and rice or beans. By planning, clipping, and shopping smart, you can save on food purchases.

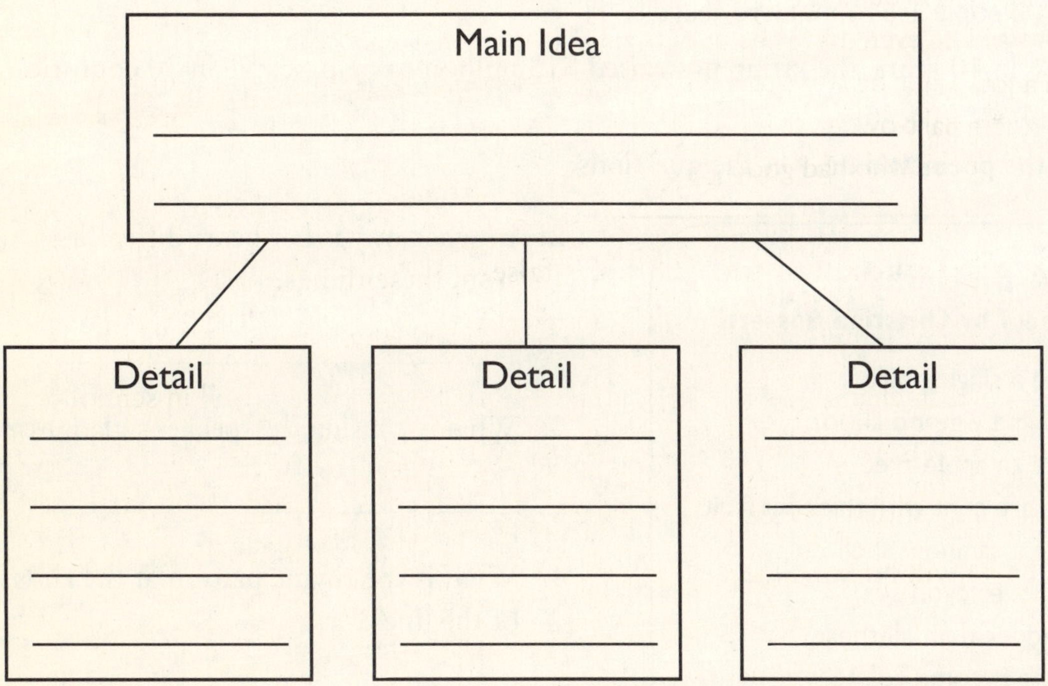

Part B Read the passage. Then circle *F* if the statement is a fact or *O* if it is an opinion.

Yellow Bins to Aid the Planet

In 1997, Planet Aid began to collect used shoes and clothing to help people in developing countries. The group set up 57 collection sites in the Boston area. It now has more than 8,000 yellow collections bins in 19 states. In its first 10 years, Planet Aid collected more than 280 million pounds of clothing. I think this proves that Americans have too much money. We should be ashamed. We have closets stuffed with clothes while some people in other countries have nothing. The United States has the world's highest per person consumption of clothing. Only about 15 percent of unwanted clothes is recycled in this country. People are too lazy to recycle. Planet Aid recycles the items that are put in their yellow bins. In 10 years, the group has raised $13 million to help people in 30 countries.

F O 1. In 1997, Planet Aid began to collect used shoes and clothing.

F O 2. The group now has collection bins in 19 states.

F O 3. I think this proves that Americans have too much money.

F O 4. We should be ashamed.

F O 5. The United States has the world's highest per person consumption of clothing.

F O 6. Only about 15 percent of unwanted clothes is recycled in this country.

F O 7. People are too lazy to recycle.

F O 8. In 10 years, the group has raised $13 million to help people in 30 countries.

Part C Read the poem and answer the questions.

A Birthday

from the poem by Christina Rossetti

My heart is like a singing bird
Whose nest is in a water'd shoot;
My heart is like an apple-tree
Whose boughs are bent with thick-set fruit;
My heart is like a rainbow shell
That paddles in a halcyon sea;
My heart is gladder than all these,
Because my love is come to me.

1. What three things does the speaker compare her heart to?

____

2. In what way is her heart different from these things?

____

3. What is causing the speaker's gladness?

____

4. What is the rhyme pattern at the ends of the lines?

____

5. How could you describe the rhythm of the poem?

____

Answer Key

Page 3

Main Idea: Everyone deserves a good source of safe water.

Detail: The water that many people drink is unclean.

Detail: Women and girls spend too much time carrying water.

Detail: In recent years, billions of dollars have been invested in water projects.

Page 4

Main Idea: Three conditions are needed to make a geyser.

Detail: Geysers must have a lot of water.

Detail: There must be a heat source.

Detail: A plumbing system must be in place.

Page 5

1. Possible answer: Wind power is becoming more important.
2. There were small increases in new wind power until 2004. From 2005 to 2007, there have been big increases.
3. Any three: Wind is a renewable energy source, it is nonpolluting, it may be cheaper than electricity produced in other ways, farmers can lease land for wind farms, it produces "green" power, and it helps Earth.
4. Possible answer: Wind power does not cause pollution, and many people want to protect Earth by reducing pollution.

Page 6

1. Possible answer: Both the American Revolution and the French Revolution were successful.
2. short-term success, long-term success, and the influence on other countries
3. It freed the 13 English colonies from Great Britain. It set up a government based on democratic ideas.
4. Several times during the 1800s, France returned to being a monarchy.
5. Latin America

Page 7

1. the artificial heart implant
2. 1969
3. 1964, 1967
4. 1962, 1969
5. 1964
6. the use of lasers
7. 1967
8. Possible answer: Both years have space-related events—one event is imaginary, and one is real.

Page 8

1. F
2. T
3. T
4. F
5. T
6. F
7. T
8. F
9. F
10. T

Page 9

Main Idea: There are several reasons why people want to protect the rain forests.

Reason 1: Rain forest plants give off 40 percent of the world's oxygen.

Reason 2: These plants take in carbon dioxide and help prevent global warming.

Reason 3: Many medicines come from rain forest plants.

Page 10

1. Wearing a helmet when riding a motorcycle saves lives and prevents serious injuries.
2. If you are not wearing a helmet when you have a motocycle accident, your hospital costs will usually be greater, your hospital stay will be longer, and your injuries will be more severe.
3. When Louisiana passed a full helmet law, deaths dropped by 30 percent the first year.
4. a helmet

Page 11

1. F
2. F
3. F
4. O
5. O
6. O
7. F
8. O

Page 12

1. F	3. F	5. B	7. F	9. B
2. F	4. B	6. B	8. B	10. B

Page 13

1. 1947 (about 14%)
2. from 1947 to about 1950
3. Inflation rose steeply, dropped steeply, and then rose again.
4. 1957–1967
5. Possible answer: Inflation is a fact of life. In general, every decade has highs and lows.

Page 14

1. Dominican Republic
2. to help overthrow a Socialist government
3. Nicaragua
4. Nicaragua, El Salvador, Honduras, and Panama
5. Possible answer: The United States has been involved in many of the Central American countries' internal conflicts.

Page 15

1. They are serious about what they are doing.
2. The men are wearing neckties under their T-shirts. Two men are carrying briefcases.
3. The causes include No Child Left Behind, Community Development Block Grant, Hubble Space Telescope, Veterans Benefits, Upward Bound, Amtrak, ANWR (Arctic National Wildlife Refuge), 2002 Farm Bill, Social Security, and Medicaid.
4. the U.S. Budget
5. Possible answer: The cartoonist thinks people should save money instead of "saving" all these causes.

Page 16

1. A man is standing in the path of several tanks.
2. A protest against the government was taking place.
3. He wants to make his point, regardless of what it costs him.
4. Possible answer: The tanks did not stop, and the man was killed.

Page 17

1. A frog is jumping into a pond.
2. sight and sound
3. silence
4. The trees are blooming, and the temple bells have stopped ringing.
5. sound and smell
6. two
7. quietness (Both poems should be read slowly and quietly so you can picture in your mind the scenes described.)
8. by using short lines and short, simple words

Page 18

1. In each stanza, lines 1 and 3 rhyme, and lines 2 and 4 rhyme.
2. In each stanza, lines 1 and 3 end with the same word.
3. The speaker was never friendly toward him.
4. after the friend dies
5. It is an old story (that is, a story often told) that we do not appreciate people until they are gone.

Page 19

1. a dog curling up and falling asleep
2. Any three of the following:

   It rubs its back or its muzzle on the window-panes.

   It licks its tongue into the corners.

   It lets soot fall on its back.

   It slips and leaps.

   It curls up and sleeps.
3. October, at night
4. yellow, rubs, window-panes
5. the "l" sound *(licked, lingered, let)*
6. the "s" sound *(slipped, sudden, seeing, soft)*

Page 20

1. An emerald is compared to grass; a ruby to blood; a sapphire to heaven.
2. Sample answer: A diamond is like a twinkling star.
3. In each stanza, lines 2 and 4 rhyme.
4. Possible answer: A flint is not a sparkling jewel; it just lies in the mud. But it is useful because it makes fires ("holds a fire").

Page 21

	Pip	the convict
Physical Description	no description	Wears grey clothes Has an iron (a chain) on his leg Has no hat, broken shoes, and a rag tied around his head Wet and muddy Cut and scratched up
How He Acts	Afraid	Is hiding in a graveyard Threatens Pip and holds him by the chin Limps, shivers, and growls
What He Says	"Don't cut my throat." Says his name is "Pip"	"Keep still, you little devil, or I'll cut your throat!" Asks what the boy's name is and where he lives
How He Says It	Pleads in terror Speaks too softly to be heard	Cries in a terrible voice

Page 22

1. It is spring. The trees are budding, and a robin is chirping.
2. It is evening. The sun is setting, and the robin seems to be chirping "Good night."
3. near hills and the sea
4. three
5. Possible answer: It is a large old home. It has a library and an extra room that was used only at Christmas, when many people came to the house.

Page 23

Characters: Kara, Emily, the doctor

Problem to Be Solved: Kara is afraid to see a doctor about a lump in her breast.

Climax: Tests prove that the lump is benign.

Conclusion: Kara takes Emily to lunch to thank her for her encouragement.

Page 24

Main character: the lieutenant

Problem to Be Solved: The lieutenant doesn't want to lose his arm.

Climax: The doctor demands that the lieutenant come with him and promises not to amputate the lieutenant's arm.

Conclusion: The lieutenant returns home, without his arm, and is embarrassed by the tears of the women in his family.

Page 25

1. Possible answer: John doesn't want Jane to use his belongings.
2. external—between John and Jane
3. with physical and verbal violence
4. She insults him.
5. Possible answer: There will be more conflicts between the cousins.

Page 26

Part A

1. F
2. T
3. F
4. T
5. F

Part B

1. Juan wants to work for his uncle, but his uncle won't hire him.
2. Juan must decide whether he is willing to work hard and improve his grades so his uncle will hire him.
3. Uncle Jorge hires Juan.
4. Possible answer: Work hard and you will succeed.

Pages 27–28, Reading Review

Part A

Main Idea: Saving requires planning, clipping, and shopping smart.

Detail: planning

Detail: clipping

Detail: shopping smart

Part B

1. F
2. F
3. O
4. O
5. F
6. F
7. O
8. F

Part C

1. a singing bird, an apple tree, and a rainbow shell
2. Her heart is even happier ("gladder") than these things.
3. Her love has come to her (line 8).
4. Lines 2 and 4 (*shoot, fruit*) rhyme, and lines 6 and 8 (*sea, me*) rhyme.
5. All the lines are about the same length, so the rhythm (or beat) is steady and even.

mhcontemporary.com

The McGraw·Hill Companies

ISBN 978007654861-3
MHID 007654861-9

McGraw Hill Contemporary